Homesteading
on the
Peace River

SECOND EDITION

OREL FELLAND
ORVILLE SEVERSON

Cover Design: Leslie Anderson
Page Layout: Zebra Graphics
Map of Trip: Martha Felland
Editor: Sonja Brown
Interior photos: Courtesy of authors
Cover and wolf photos: Shutterstock
Photo Enhancement: Marc Felland

Emails: SonjaBrown62@gmail.com
        Rob@robseverson.com

ISBN 978-1-105-77254-2

Printed in the United States of America.

Contents

Introduction   1

Chapter 1: On to Peace River   5

Chapter 2: We Are Homesteaders   13

Chapter 3: The Irishman   21

Chapter 4: Our Cabin   29

Chapter 5: Dan the Lumberjack   35

Chapter 6: The Trapper   39

Chapter 7: Defeat at the Bluff   49

Chapter 8: The Last Summer   57

Chapter 9: Back to the U.S.A.   65

Epilogue   73

About the Authors   80

Introduction

T he story by these two young men who became homesteaders in northern Canada unfolds in the year 1928 in the town of Harmony, Minnesota, just prior to the Great Depression. Getting a job was difficult, and many people found themselves having to be creative and willing to take whatever work they could find. Thus it was that Orel and Orville, both just twenty-one years old, ended up going first to the Canadian province of Saskatchewan and eventually into the wilderness of northern Alberta to try their hand at homesteading in Peace River country.

Orville Severson (left) and Orel Felland.

Peace River is both the name of a great river and the name of a small town established in the river valley in the early 1900s by immigrants from many different countries. The river is a huge Arctic stream formed thousands of years ago by the melting of Glacial Lake Peace. Its name, which means "big river" in the Cree language, derives from a settlement between warring parties of the Cree and Beaver Indian tribes in about 1781, according to an online article by David W. Leonard. The 1,923 kilometers-long (about 1,200 miles) river flows east from the Rocky

Mountains of British Columbia, then north, and then east again into Lake Athabaska.

In the early twentieth century, this country was true wilderness where only the hardy could survive. Fur trappers, gold prospectors, and homesteaders traded the rigors of forty-to-sixty degrees below zero, the devastating fight with mosquitoes, sweeping blizzards, marauding wolf packs and bears, and twenty-hour-long nights of darkness for the chance of a new life in this rugged country. Had Orville and Orel known just how harrowing their adventures would be, they might not have left their comfortable farming community in Harmony, but they were young and optimistic, and despite their struggles likely would not have exchanged the experience of living in "the Peace" for anything.

—*Sonja Brown, Editor, Second Edition*
Ken Torgerson, Editor, First Edition

Chapter 1

On to Peace River

By Orel

In the year 1928 I was working for Tostin Applen for fifty dollars a month with my time to be up on September first. Threshing was about over. In the meantime, Roger Engle and I had been talking about going to North Dakota to work in the harvest fields, so I got Bill Sears to take my place at Tostin's to finish the threshing, which would take about two days. Tostin was in poor health and he was not able to haul bundles.

Saturday night we left in a 1926 Model T roadster, took in the state fair on Sunday, and then left for Fargo, North Dakota. We got there on Monday in time to go to the employment office, where we learned that a man named John Yidstie wanted two men to help with threshing. He lived east of Hillsboro, North Dakota, in the Red River Valley. We got there late in the evening and hired out to him for four dollars for an eleven-hour day.

We threshed about five days before it started to rain, and it rained and rained. We got our meals but no wages yet, and we got so tired of laying around that we did the milking and chores. The Yidstie women were real pleased with this, as there were no boys in the family, so they had been doing the chores. For our help they washed our clothes. It finally quit raining after about two weeks, and Roger and I reshocked ninety acres of oats that were starting to grow.

When that was done, Mr. Yidstie said, "We'll get a good start in the morning." We went to bed early and at four o'clock a rap at the bunkhouse woke us. There was John Yidstie, and he said, "What do you think it's doing? It's raining." So no work for three or four days, we thought.

We asked for our pay that morning and left for Hillsboro. Driving on gumbo dirt roads, the wheels picked up so much mud they would hardly turn, but we got to town and I called my uncle in Craik, Saskatchewan, and asked if he could use two men. He said to come right away as they were just going to start their harvesting and they had a big crop.

We started out and got to Winnipeg late in the afternoon, then continued on to Brandon. It had been a long dusty trip so we slept in the depot for a few hours, then got started for my uncle's place. We were really tired when we finally arrived at Craik, but we found the farm about nine o'clock that evening. After a good meal and a long visit, we were introduced to the movable bunkhouse, which was on wheels. It was about ten feet wide and about twenty feet long with upper and lower berths on each end. All of the bunks were solid board platforms with straw over them. The bottom bunks were right on the floor and you had to supply your own pillow and blanket.

There were lots of sweaty and gassy odors floating about in this mobile bunkhouse. About half of us talked English, so we stayed on one side and the Russians, Poles, or Hungarians, or whatever stayed on the other side. A

Henry and John Sanden's threshing rig in 1928. Orel and Roger Engle worked with the crew. The bunkhouse and the cook car are in the rear, with the cow on behind for milk. Heat for the engine was obtained by burning straw. They worked with this threshing rig for 46 days, setting a record for threshing oats: 7,200 bushels in 12 hours. Ten men hauled the bundles to the rig and two extra men pitched bundles into the machine.

The threshing rig in operation.

The tank wagon used to haul water for the steam engine.

small stove and a bench in the middle was about all the furniture, so you washed in the horse trough, sometimes breaking the ice to get at the water. We had to get up at four bells in the morning, then harness and feed our two horses. There were ten men to haul in the bundles of grain, and Roger and I were two of these ten. Breakfast was at five o'clock after we had put in an hour's work.

They started threshing at about a quarter to six when it was yet dark, and we hauled several loads before sunrise. They brought us some lunch about nine and then we worked until noon. Without much rest we started threshing again until about a quarter to one, then ate a lunch at four, and kept on working until about seven-thirty, which made it a darn long day.

Several of the men wore blood-stained rags on their hands for gloves until their hands got toughened in. Our hands were used to tough work so no problems. We threshed for about forty days like this, long hours, but we could take it as then we were young and strong.

My uncle liked to move the threshing rig about sundown and then start a new straw pile and set the old pile on fire so that we could see better. It was very hard work, but there were rewards when we stretched out after supper. The prairie moon is really a beautiful thing to see as it moves up over the horizon, and I would like to have a recording of the night sounds. There were the coyotes howling, the crunch, crunch of the horses chewing, the steam engine sizzling, and the great snores from tired bodies.

We had the bunkhouse on wheels wherever we threshed out in the fields, so we didn't get to town or into a house for almost six weeks. There were three or four dogs hanging around to get scraps from the cook shack, which was also on wheels. There was an old-fashioned cook stove in one end plus a small cupboard and a table for eighteen men. Food was good, as there was a plentiful supply of meat and potatoes and vegetables. Mrs. Labot was the cook. She was strong enough to pick up a hundred pounds of flour and walk up the steps into the cook shack. She could shoulder a quarter of beef with no problem. She had a young girl to help her, and the meals were always on time. These women slept on a mattress in the cook shack.

When the work was over and we had finished the threshing, I returned to Harmony for the winter. I had visited my other uncle, John, in Canada and he said he would like to have me come back in the spring and work for him. My Uncle Henry wanted a man too, so I talked Orville Severson into going with me the next spring and that was the start of a whole new adventure.

We left Minnesota by train on the fifteenth of April in 1929 and arrived in Saskatchewan on the twentieth. There had been no snow that winter and it was exceptionally dry all that summer. A little sprinkle came down in June and then no rain until after harvest time. My Uncle Henry had seeded 2,000 acres of wheat and got only 4,000 bushels back for all his labors, which was not much over 1,200 bushels more than he had seeded.

Uncle John had a hired hand by the name of Bill

Cummings, a Scotsman. He had homesteaded in the Peace River country of northern Alberta the year before, and all he talked about was the good country up there. For seasonal workers, the job was over on October 10th, so at that time Bill took his money and bought an old team, a cow, and a wagon. My Uncle John also gave him some old machinery, which with his other possessions, we loaded onto a special immigrant car at Craik that offered a really cheap homesteader's rate.

I had $254 for my summer's wages and had spent only nine dollars that whole summer, even buying a pair of shoes out of the nine bucks. I had also paid my life insurance, which was $64.25. Orville and I caught the homesteader's fever from Bill Cummings, I guess, and had decided to head for Peace River country with him. I sneaked into one of the railroad cars at night and got myself back under the machinery where the yard inspector wouldn't see me. He inspected the load but never spied me so I had a free ride all the way. Bill had bought a ticket, and Orville planned to hitchhike with some other immigrants. We were to meet at Peace River.

The train came to a halt at Saskatoon, and the car that I was on stopped right in front of the yard inspector's headquarters. The cops on the railroad were called "yard bulls" and I had heard that they were the meanest bunch of guys. Bill Cummings stayed in his car as he was a paid passenger, but I was still hiding back under the machinery where I laid for 23 hours, not daring to show myself. The engines finally picked us up, and Bill's carload was the first car. When they started up, I thought this car would be pulled in two as there were over one hundred cars on behind. It turned out to be a slow, slow ride. After we got past Edmonton, there were lots of muskeg swamps that we passed over, which were very soft and spongy.

At Smith, a town near Lesser Slave Lake, there must have been over a hundred men who climbed onto different cars of the train, men who most likely were going north to find a place for the winter. When we got to Nampa, a very small town eighteen miles southeast of Peace River, Bill's car was sidetracked. I helped him unload and take all of his possessions out to his homestead, which took us a couple of days.

Bill and I then hitched up the team and started for Peace River, but on the way who should we meet but Orville! The Postmaster and storekeeper at Nampa had been a former neighbor of my Uncle John's. His name was Shorty Brown. He had sent word to the Postmaster at Peace River that we were there at Bill Cumming's place. Orville had just happened to ask him if a letter was there for him, so the word got to Orville and he came out to meet us at the homestead.

Chapter 2

We Are Homesteaders
By Orel

B ill turned the horses around, and we went back to his place where we stayed for several days. From there Orville and I walked all over the area looking for a homestead, but all we could find was a place covered with very heavy timber, mostly pine and poplar, and it was a long ways from the road.

We walked to Peace River and checked at the land office for available plots. We found two quarter-sections side by side, located about ten miles from Peace River. The land agent told us that they were good homesteads—near North Star and Natakew, which was north of Fairview sixteen miles northwest of Peace River. We caught several rides and got to Fairview, then started to walk to North Star. Along the way there was an Indian settlement and they had some horses, so we asked if we could use two of them to go to North Star. We made a deal of a dollar for each pony, but we had to be back the next evening.

We put the Army saddles on the ponies and took off in a steady jog, which is a pace between a walk and a fast trot. We rode until evening and found a small haystack back in the bush at .the edge of a clearing. We built a small fire, had some tea and bread with peanut butter, then rolled up in our blankets and went to sleep.

This was October in northern Alberta and you just don't forget about the weather if you know what's good for you. A sinister freeze can slide in on you during the night, as it did for us. We crawled deeper into the hay trying to gain as much warmth as possible. When we woke up in the morning, I had Orville's cap partly on and he had mine, which was bigger and fitted down over his ears. We looked at each other and had to laugh. One of the ponies was gone, but we could trace his tracks in the frost that whitened the landscape. We found the pony at a Russian homestead about a mile away. The owners could not speak English, but they were glad to see somebody and gave us a good lunch. Through sign language we found out that there were three more families coming to settle in the area. We thanked them for their generosity and rode off to survey this part of the country. We spent considerable time looking over the land that was available, then returned the ponies to the Indians and walked back to Peace River. We had made up our minds. We filed on the two homesteads southeast of town, which were about ten miles deep into the bush.

We bought a B.C. camp stove, some granite dishes, several blankets and pillows, and started keeping house in an abandoned schoolhouse that had no windows. From there we could walk to our homestead. It didn't take us long to find an ideal place to build our cabin, right on the section line. It had a pocket of poplars and thick spruce trees all around. The trees we started cutting for our cabin walls were large and very heavy to handle but we managed and began building by putting the biggest

Bill Cummings at Peace River 1930.

logs on the bottom. It was our first experience building a log house. It was fourteen feet by sixteen feet with a dirt roof. You make the roof by placing heavy poles very close together for the rafters and then laying lengthwise some spruce boughs covered with slough grass. We covered the slough grass with about ten to twelve inches of dirt to make sure our roof would not leak.

When the main structure was up, the next step was to chink, or put moss in, the cracks between the logs. Winter was here already and it was turning colder, so we decided to quit for the day. We put the moss inside the cabin and dug a cellar, which was four by four by four feet, in the center of the room. We had been staying at the old abandoned schoolhouse while we built our own place, and headed back there for the night. We could feel that the temperature was really dropping. We cut hitch rails and some more wood for the night and nailed what clothes we could spare over the window openings. We moved our bed next to the stove and hit the sack with our clothes on.

We fired the stove all night but we were so cold that we got up at 4:30 and made oatmeal for breakfast, which turned out pretty thin, and it froze before we had finished eating. We made up some sandwiches for lunch and started out for our new cabin.

When we got there our hands were so cold that when we took off our mittens, we could hardly start a fire. The moss was frozen solid, so we piled it around our little cellar and moved the fire down into the pit so the moss would thaw out.

We chinked the walls starting at the top and by the time we were at the bottom logs, we had to lay on our stomachs. Our mittens got soaked from the wet moss. After a long day, we started out for the old schoolhouse.

Our clothes were not the greatest. I had only a pair of shoes and rubbers and one pair of socks. Orville was a little better off, as he had brought a pair of shoe packs and two pairs of wool socks. The cold was penetrating, it seemed, right down to our bones, and my feet were very cold as we walked the road back to our flimsy "shack" for the night.

We passed by Emerson Brown's cabin on the way. We were acquainted with them as we had helped with their threshing for two days. Mrs. Brown was a plump, kindly lady, and she saw us going by. She hailed us down and said, "You're not going to that old cabin tonight. You guys come in and stay here with us, and no arguments about it."

I said, "Well, it's pretty cold tonight," and she replied, "You bet it is. It's 55 below zero."

When I took my shoes and socks off, both my feet were frozen pretty bad. During the following winters for about seven years after that, if I wasn't careful in the cold my feet would break open in several places. I had to wear felt shoes all winter, and sometimes that was hardly enough to protect them.

We stayed at Browns' place for a night and a day and then used his team to move our stuff to our new cabin. The weather warmed up some, and we put our floor in and made a bunk bed out of poles. We made a kitchen table and cut more wood to burn, which took us about a week's time. While getting our cabin livable, we got acquainted with our Hungarian neighbor we called "Steve" and also visited another neighbor who went by the name of "Henry."

Our cabin was pretty snug now, so we had time to do some hunting. We shot a few snowshoe rabbits and some grouse. We also tried out melting some snow for washing dishes. There were bugs in it but we would strain them out. Good water in the Peace River country was a premium commodity, so in the winter melted snow made good tea and coffee water and had other uses as well.

We hardly ever worked on Thursdays as it was mail day. One Thursday we walked to town, visited Rosy's

This was the log house where Orel and Orville stayed when they cut wood for Lyle Barker.

Orel and Orville standing in front of their first cabin at Peace River.

Tobacco Shop, had a cup of tea at Niggles Restaurant and were walking toward the store when our Hungarian neighbor Steve saw us. He waved his arms wildly at us, and when we got up to him jabbered a mile a minute in Hungarian. We couldn't understand him but another fellow came along and interpreted for him.

It seems a bear had gotten into our homestead cabin and had strewn everything around, tipped our stove over, tore the bunk apart, and had dragged our trunk outside, which contained our tea, coffee, sugar, and other items. The bear didn't get the trunk open, but our flour was all over everything. What a mess. We had been staying near town and hadn't been out there for a month while we were cutting another supply of wood. On Sunday we went back out again and we figured that the invading bear had been a female. She had been back again with her two cubs, which were about half-grown. We knew better than to fool around with a female bear with young. We didn't try to track her. We just cleaned up and fixed the damaged cabin.

Chapter 3

The Irishman

By Orel

There was an Irishman living south of us who would stop in every Thursday on mail day. One day he said, "I'm a dammer. Don't you need a cook?" We talked to Barkers, and they said yes if he would cook for his board, so he got the job. At the same time, Lyle also got a fellow by the name of DeLance to help him haul the wood for us.

Don Leahy was the Irishman's name, and he talked and told stories all the time. He nicknamed DeLance "Stumblefoot," a name that stuck with him. We also had a mixed-race Indian by the name of Johnny Poquet to help us cut wood. He was only sixteen years old, but he was a good addition to our crew.

Lyle brought home an accordion, and Johnny fooled around with it for several evenings until he got so he could play a tune. Later that winter he learned to play a violin somewhat for our entertainment, as one needed diversions in this far north country. The days are very short in the winter when you are only 800 miles south of the Arctic Circle. The sun rises at about ten to ten-thirty in the morning and sets at about two-thirty in the afternoon. The summers, of course, are the opposite with hardly any darkness in June, so in the winter there was plenty of time to read, sharpen your tools, or busy yourself with other tasks.

Dan was a good housekeeper and cook and besides that, he had a great sense of humor. The group of us were invited to a wedding reception up the road a ways, so we dressed up in the best clothes we had and walked to the party. The groom had wine and cigars to pass around. Dan liked to be in the middle of things, so he passed the cigars first. He came to a bachelor homesteader and offered him a cigar. Clifford was his name.

Cliff said, "I don't smoke."

Dan finished with the cigars and started to pass out the wine. When he came to Cliff, Cliff said, "I don't drink."

Dan then said, "I'm a goddammer. Do you eat hay?"

Cliff said, "No, I don't."

Dan replied, "Man, you are not fit company for man nor beast."

****

It would be an understatement to say that it was cold that first winter. We had a kitchen stove and a wood heater, and on the coldest nights someone would stay up and fire the stoves. It was all poplar or soft wood, which doesn't give off very much heat and burns up real fast. Whoever stayed up would go to bed about midnight or later, leaving water boiling on the stove to create a little additional heat. When we woke up in the morning, the water would be frozen solid on the stove.

One evening Lyle came home at about four o'clock. He had caught a ride to town and some way or another had heard the news that there was to be a house party and dance eight miles south of us. It was about sixty degrees below zero at six that evening. Lyle drained the kerosene out of the truck's radiator, and it was so cold that it would hardly run out. We put it on the stove and got the kerosene boiling, then put it back in the radiator. With the starter going and the help of a crank, we could almost turn the motor over. We heated the kerosene and put it back into the radiator three more times. No luck. Finally, we hooked our team of horses in front, but the back wheels slid so we built a fire under the rear end to heat the frozen grease. We got the kerosene boiling again and with Orville on the crank, I drove the team in front and Lyle steered the truck. It started.

We left for the dance, and by now it was more than sixty degrees below. We got to the dance and really had a great time, although every half-hour Lyle had to go out and start the truck to warm it up.

There was a group there from Little Prairie, about seven or eight miles east, who came with a team and a sled. We danced until one o'clock and what fun we had. We sang "God Save the Queen" and said goodnight. One of the boys with the team went to hitch them up, and he found both horses dead. They laid in the barn with pools of blood frozen from their nostrils. Their lungs had frozen or been damaged. It really bothered me. If the horses had just been walked a few times it probably would never have happened.

A sleigh pulls hard when the temperature drops to fifty degrees below or colder, so we had learned to stop the horses if they started to breathe hard. We built a "caboose" on the sled with a little stove in it, which made it real nice for going to and from work. It was also a handy place to eat our lunch when it was very cold. We usually didn't go to the woods if it was lower than forty below, but sometimes before we would get home at night it would drop below that.

One morning we got up and looked out and saw water dripping from the roof. When we had gone to bed, it had been below zero. This was our first and only experience with the warm chinook wind. It thawed all day, and the temperature rose to forty-five degrees above. That night we went to bed with only a small fire burning. At about four in the morning one of us woke up, and it was below zero in the cabin. The temperature had dropped to forty below outside. Our warm weather had disappeared fast.

Lyle Barker had a younger brother, age seventeen, still trying to get through grade school. In northern Alberta the school vacation takes place during December and January because of the short days and long periods of darkness. Lyle's brother's name was Alphonse. He was six feet tall and in the fourth grade. He had been sent out to live with us because he was not getting along very well in town.

The school teacher was a man from England, who was six-and-a-half feet tall. He had only one leg as the other one had been shot off in World War I. He was a very good teacher, and he could handle Alphy. Dan nicknamed Alphy "the Punk." Punk would not do a thing but eat. Dan prepared his lunch for noon, and Dan would say, "I'm a goddammer. I loaded his pail to the gunnels, and it always comes home empty."

When spring came, our pond ended up with a layer of water on top of the ice. Dan rigged up a fishing pole and made some doughballs. He told Punk to catch some fish for supper, although we all knew there were no fish in the pond. It was kind of a dirty trick, but Dan would keep looking out the door and laugh every time he saw Punk sitting there with his hands grasping the pole tightly, waiting for a bite.

During the spring I helped Barker put his crop in. He had rented land, and Lyle and I finally got the seeding done. He had an 18-36 Hart Par pulling a bottom plow. At this time, Orville got a job driving a small cat clearing land.

We wanted to abandon our claim and buy some other land. We found a friend of Steve's that would give us thirty-five dollars for the right to file on our claim, so we went to the land office and I filled out the paperwork to abandon the claim. The other fellow who wanted it stood right behind me and filed on our land. We then purchased 320 acres of land about five miles from Peace River. This land had about two acres cleared off. This former homestead was along the road called the Groured Trail. The name came from a priest who had gathered about 300 men and women to start a settlement and a Catholic mission at Peace River. They had started out from Edmonton in 1890 with a sawmill, flour mill, and many wagons and horses. They brought cows for milk, and it took them all summer to get to the Peace River area. A large group of men went ahead of the wagons to chop down trees and make a trail.

I lived in a tent on our new land during the month of June. I planted two acres of potatoes and cleared some land, cutting poles and logs for our new cabin. If you thought Minnesota mosquitoes were bad, you have never seen the likes of them along the Peace River. At night we would try to smudge out the tent, then close it as tight as we could. Several mornings I counted as many as fifty-eight of them full of blood and waiting for the darkness to come so they could gorge themselves again. The homesteaders who had cattle would make a pole fence about twenty feet square and build a fire in the evening, then throw green brush on it, and the cattle would stand in the smoke. Many oxen and horses would run away in desperation, trying to evade the swarms of thousands that surrounded their bodies.

About the first of July I got a job driving a big Allis Chalmers with a breaking plow. I would start to work at two in the morning and drive until one the next afternoon. Another fellow, a Cockney Englishman, would run the tractor until eleven in the evening. We each were paid two dollars a day and could plow about five to six acres during this time. The plow took a twenty-two-inch cut, and we plowed about eight to ten inches deep. This land had been cleared of timber, and we would hit a lot of stumps—not too big, but they would stop the tractor dead. We would back up and hit the stump again, and sometimes we couldn't get through the second time.

I worked at this until harvest time, when I started to run a threshing rig for Gilbert Oxford. He had a wife named Maude. Gilbert had advertised for a woman from England, and Maude had answered the ad. He sent his picture and other data, and she accepted his offer of marriage so he paid for her passage. They were very nice people. Maude and a sister had run a bake shop in South Hampton, England, so she was a very good cook.

Times were now getting harder due to the terrible Depression across the country. Prices for wheat and oats were cheap. Oats were seven to eight cents per bushel, and wheat was about thirty-five cents at Peace River, which is a long way from any grain terminal. Freight costs were very high in proportion to the price of grain.

Orville finished his job, and I was through with the threshing also. Oxford didn't have any money to pay my wages because he had bank payments to make so they wouldn't take his machinery. To make up for this, he gave me some pork, bacon, and eggs.

Orel with a bear he shot in 1930 in Harmony Valley, an unincorporated community in northern Alberta.

A group of neighbors at Peace River. Orel is second from the left and Orville is fifth from the left of those standing.

Chapter 4

Our Cabin

By Orel

Wе returned to the land we had purchased and proceeded to construct our second cabin, which was fourteen feet wide by sixteen feet long. We bought some cheap lumber for a floor, along with a door and a window, and when the walls were up, we made our roof similar to the one on our first cabin of poles, pine boughs, slough grass, and dirt. The roof was about a foot thick and it was a good insulator against the cold. It never leaked.

When finished, the cabin was very warm and pleasant. We didn't dig our potatoes soon enough, and one night the ground froze about two inches deep. We thought the potatoes would be all right and sold them to the store in Peace River where our friends Bob Claughton and Mrs. Barker worked. We rented a team of horses, hauled two big wagon loads to town, and put the potatoes in the basement of the store. But in a week they started to spoil and stink, so we had to get the wagon and horses again to haul them to the dump—a bad experience, financially and otherwise. Two acres of spoiled potatoes and no income.

By this time we had made a lot of friends. There were dances at times in Peace River, and we would put our shoes in our jacket pockets or a sack and walk to the dance. Everybody wore moccasins with wool socks and rubbers over them. If it was real cold we did not use rubbers, for if you kept moving or walking, your feet would stay warm regardless.

On mail day if it was real cold, you would see a team of horses plodding along with everybody walking behind. If it was fifty degrees below zero or colder, you could hear the sled and harness chains clinking over a mile away. We could talk to our neighbor, Wes Lane, at least a half-mile away in a normal voice. When you got to the top of the hill above Peace River, you were about 700 feet above the town, which was two miles away. The smoke from every chimney would go straight up and looked like white threads hanging from the sky. At the height of the hill, the smoke would level off.

The second winter Orville and I cut trees and brush from thirty acres of our land. We piled it in windrows so that we could burn all the branches and bushes and other debris. One evening after work we were invited to Browns' cabin for a Salvation Army revival. Orville and I went to it, and they had a song fest and some lectures. The leader was young and could play a banjo and sing very well. Mrs. Brown gave us lunch and we left for home with the young Salvation Army man walking with us. He was going back to Peace River, but he was not dressed for the cold like we were so we asked him to stay all night.

Our one bed was built in the corner. It was six feet wide and seven feet long, filled with straw and very comfortable, we thought. The young man slept in the middle. When we woke up in the morning, he was sitting by the table fully dressed. He said, "How can you sleep in that bed? There are mice in the straw."

There *were* mice in the straw, but they didn't bother us any. Eventually, though, we got a half-grown black and white cat to deal with the mice. She was a lot of fun but would make a mess in the cabin. Orville had heard that after a cat made a mess, you should stick its nose in it and put the cat outside. We left a window partly open for her to get out, but she wouldn't mind us. Orville would stick her nose in the mess, then put her out the window, but he never got her house-broken. All she would do was do her "job." Orville would stick her nose in it, and she would jump out the window.

****

We had an Italian neighbor, an immigrant, who talked very broken English. He was a large raw-boned man who had been a miner in Italy, and he was very strong and especially hot-headed. The support pole, or beam, in our cabin roof sagged from the weight of the dirt layer, and that bothered him. He said that he was going to jack it up, so he cut a pole the right height from the floor and then made two long thinly tapered wedges. He started the thin side of one wedge under the pole and the other wedge from the opposite side. He tapped them with a maul we had. He kept tapping, and the beam was getting straighter. He had raised the beam about four inches and was going to give the beam one last tap. He missed the wedge and hit the pole, and it popped away. One end hit him on the head, and he lost his temper and threw the maul through our nice double window. He left us, swearing. The beam still sagged, and we had to replace our window.

The Italian called us "Orleans" and "Marvels." One day he asked Marvels if he would help him with his Ford to go down the Peace River road into town. The bands in a Model T would only last four or five trips down and up the Peace River hill, which was about two miles long, so Orville said yes, he would help. This Italian's name was Victor Premo Peterlano. We called him "Wick" for short. Orville was supposed to step on the brake pedal, and Wick on the low gear pedal and the reverse pedal.

Wick said, "Marvels, ven I holler, you step on da brake goin' down da hill."

Away they went, and Wick yelled, and Orville stepped on the brake, but nothing happened and Wick kept hollering. Wick had very large feet, and when Orville stepped down on the brake pedal, it was on Wick's little toe, which had a corn on it. Finally, Wick saw a spot where he might be able to get the Ford stopped. He turned the Model T into a bank and came to a dead stop. He made a grab for Orville, but Orville got away from him and ran up the hill. Wick couldn't catch him. After a while, Wick's temper cooled off, and the two of them sat down and talked it over.

Wick liked pine squirrels, which are smaller than the common gray squirrels. He would hunt until he had nine or ten, then skin them and split them, head and all. Using a piece of sharpened stick, he would pick the brain and the little tongue out. One day, it had been raining while he was hunting, so he got real wet. When he came home, he built a real hot fire in the stove to dry his clothes. The top of his stove was very thin metal and would get red-hot. He took off his overalls and hung them above the stove, feeling them now and then to see if they were dry. By doing this, he dislodged some bullets, which dropped out onto the hot stove and exploded, sending lead flying.

He came running toward our cabin, shouting, "I'm shots, I'm shots, I'm shots!"

He was in his underwear, which had some blood on it, so we gave him an overall to put on and drove him in his Model T to the doctor's office in Peace River. All the doc could find was a furrow where one of the shell casings had creased him.

****

Wick bought a team of horses, but he kept them on the land he had, which was about seven miles away. The place he lived across from us was only temporary. One day he came over and said, "I sharpa my horses." We couldn't understand this until he pointed to his big feet and said, "I sharpa my horses." We finally got the idea that he had shoed his horses. When he would turn his horses out in the pasture, he would always say, "I throw my horses loose to grass."

Chapter 5

Dan the Lumberjack
By Orel

Wick got his cabin built and also a little barn, then left the area, and we didn't see him anymore. Rosy Macalroy owned the property where Wick had lived, and there was a lot of timber on it—big pines, poplar, and diamond willow with several patches of grassy meadows. Everything was bone dry, as it hadn't rained for weeks.

One day Macalroy said to Orville and me, "If you drop a match in the grass on my land, I will make it worth your while." Well, we did, and the fire took off. It got into the pines, which looked like oil wells were burning. This scared us, and we took off for home. We had left some timber standing on our property for wind breaks, and we stayed there, anxiously watching the great billows of smoke roar into the sky.

It seemed like only thirty minutes before two red-coated Canadian Mounties came by to see us. We were really scared now. They asked us if we knew how the fire got started, but we pleaded innocence. I don't think they believed us, but they said we had better get busy and protect Wes Lane's property, which was down the road about half a mile. Wes was our neighbor, so of course we would help.

I don't think Orville and I ever put in a worse day, but we saved Lane's buildings. We were sick from the smoke and still afraid that the Mounties would again be after us. The fire burned off great areas of timber, and we heard it had gone east for over thirty miles. The only consolation we got was knowing that it would save a lot of work for the homesteaders who were clearing their land. But, never again. Justice is swift and certain in Canada.

****

We helped our friend Dan Leahy build a small house on his homestead out of some lumber he had stored. It turned out to be a very nice shack. A man by the name of LeGrew, who was about sixty years old—around the same age as Dan—had a homestead west of Dan's place about a mile away. Dan loved people and company, so Dan and LeGrew decided they would live together, three months at LeGrew's and three months at Dan's. That way, they could "prove up" on the land, as the homesteading law stated that you had to have thirty acres cleared and ten acres in crops.

So, we helped Dan move in with LeGrew. Dan was Irish Catholic. At two o'clock in the morning we were roused by a knock on the door. There was Dan, all worked up, and muttering to himself. I said, "What's the matter, Dan?"

Dan replied, "LeGrew is an Orangeman, and that is the group of Protestants who are fighting the Irish Catholics in Ireland."

We had to move Dan's stuff out of LeGrew's and back to his home, and he wouldn't even go with us, but we didn't mind too much as Dan was good company.

That same winter, Dan would wake us up at four or five in the morning on mail day. His first words were usually something like, "I'm a goddammer, yee will get bed sores laying in bed all the time."

Dan had a five-mile walk to get to our place, and he was always welcome. Many times he would tell us stories about his youth on the railroad gangs and the logging operations in northern Minnesota. His folks also had worked on the building of the Canadian railroads, and they had to work five years, he said, just to pay for their passage from Ireland. His dad had been a day laborer on the track gangs, and his mother was a cook.

Dan had worked in northern Minnesota during the "hey days" of the lumberjack years, 1908 through 1916. The crews would cut and skid logs to the banks of the Kettle and Snake rivers, and a lot of logs had to be hauled by logging sleds, which were very large and heavy. The sleds were six feet between the runners with an eight-foot bolster, and it took four to six horses just to keep them going after they got started. They used twelve to sixteen horses to start the load, and a man with a water wagon would put water in the sled tracks to make the sled pull easier, as there would be from 10,000 to 15,000 board feet of lumber on each load.

The horses were shod with steel shoes with very sharp calks. When they started downhill, the horses had to run at full speed to keep ahead of the sled. Going uphill would be a terrific pull and strain on the horses. Both horses and men were sometimes killed on the downhill run, which was always extremely dangerous.

Dan said he saw the record load hauled on a sled, which was 23,000 board feet of pine. He had a picture of it. The logs would be stacked on the river bank, and when the spring floods came, the lumberjacks would break the logs loose and get them into the water so that they would be on their way to the sawmill.

Some "Jacks" would ride the logs and keep them from jamming up on a bend in the river. Those men who couldn't ride the logs would stand at critical locations and keep the logs in the mainstream. Sometimes logs were lost, but most of them usually arrived at the sawmill.

The first thing the lumberjacks would do when they "hit" town was to get a good bath, a haircut, and some new clothes. Jacks usually had a pocket full of money and were out for a good time. In their way, they managed to have one. Dan said they would get a few drinks and then the fights would begin, which many times ended up with everything in the saloon getting smashed. The next day they would all come back and pay the whole damage bill, as they were an honest, hard-working, and very strong-willed lot of men. They had been cooped up all winter, and this was their release for their emotions.

Dan said one of the favorite challenges of these daredevil men was that one would take his jacket off and drag it behind him, daring anyone to step on it. If somebody did, there was a fight to the finish, and the last thing a victor would do was to step on the loser's face with his hob-nailed boots to mark him.

Chapter 6

The Trapper
By Orville

T he winter day in northern Alberta comes slowly. We busied ourselves in the kerosene lantern light by sharpening the axes and saws. Three years had passed since we had left home, and now we were fairly comfortable in our snug cabin built on the land we had purchased. Game was plentiful. Prairie chickens, partridge, snowshoe rabbits, moose, and deer along with our own supply of potatoes made life fairly easy during the long winter. We also had a good supply of staple items such as salt, sugar, and coffee.

About 9 o'clock the first light of dawn appeared. I wrapped my blistered hand carefully, but the pain seemed deeper this morning. We trudged out through the snow to where we had been clearing the land and began chopping, trimming, and pulling the trees into windrows so we could burn them. By 10 o'clock the sun moved above the horizon, and we worked at a steady pace to get as much done as possible before the light faded away around 2:30. My hand ached more severely, and the pain and redness seemed to be moving up my arm.

Orel said, "Orville, I think you've got blood poisoning. You've got to get to a doctor."

We hiked the ten miles to Peace River, and they put me to bed in the large log house they called the hospital. With bed rest and proper care, my infection receded in about ten days.

While I was recuperating, they brought in a trapper from the north, downriver. He looked very bad, suffering, I understood, from a severe case of inflammatory rheumatism. His feet were so tender the nurses couldn't put a sheet on them. As he gradually improved, he became very friendly and talked about his struggle to get here from the trappers' cabin fifty miles into the back country.

His name was Cy Wilson. He told how his trapping partners had built a crude sled from rope and wood slats and how they tied him to the sled and let him slide down about one hundred feet over the side of a steep bluff from the cabin down to the frozen river bank. They packed him warmly on the sled and then began the long ordeal of pulling the sick trapper through the deep snow. The temperature was forty below zero, not unusual for the Peace River country, which has the coldest average temperatures on the North American continent except for the North Slope of Alaska and the high plateaus of Nova Scotia.

The two trappers made fifteen miles the first day struggling with the crude sled, but the terrific strain on their young and rugged bodies wore them down to exhaustion. Then they laid through the bitter and long night huddled together for warmth. They decided the next day they must have help, so one of the men hiked ahead ten miles to an Indian's cabin, where they might find a dog team and sled. They were indeed lucky to get the sturdy huskies and the help of the Indian. They mushed back to the sick trapper and carefully placed him in the sled. After two days, they made it to the town of Peace River, but every swerve and bump had put Cy in terrific pain.

After he had recovered enough to move about, he came out to our cabin to more fully recover as we had invited him several times. He stayed with us for some time, eating well and sleeping and regaining his strength. At last he got itchy to rejoin his trapper friends down the river to the north, so he thought he could leave. I didn't feel like letting him go alone on foot for fifty miles in this bitter cold, so I said I would hike along with him, never realizing at the time what I was letting myself in for. We made up our shoulder packs, dressed as warmly as we could, and took off downriver. The snow was deep, making progress difficult, but we made considerable distance the first day.

We had made it to an Indian cabin and stayed with them the first night, got some extra food, and left before daylight as we wanted to make it to the next cabin twenty miles away. We made a lot of miles before daylight, and at noon we stopped, built a fire, melted snow in a gallon can, and boiled some black tea. Our lunch and the hot tea picked us up a little, and we trudged on. As we plodded along through the deep snow, we came upon a dead moose, which the timber wolves had killed and had only half-eaten. The wolves hunt in packs, and they know better than to get too close to the deadly front feet of a moose. Some of the wolves distract the moose in front while others will come from behind and pull him down by slashing his tendons with their sharp teeth. The moose goes down on his back legs and is helpless. It looked to us like they ate his hind quarter while he was still alive as there was blood spewed everywhere. We were glad we had our knives and the extra box of shells when we saw the size of those wolf tracks. We made it to the cabin shortly after dark, and by this time it was getting bitterly cold. The cabin was a good one, and the last people there had left kindling and wood for the stove. We soon had a good fire and some light from a piece of cloth laying in grease drippings. It was really smoky, but we could see to cook up some supper. To one wall there were bunks and some blankets, so it was a pretty comfortable place under the circumstances.

I was wearing three pair of heavy wool socks inside of low rubbers. Cy had the same. Wearing shoes and overshoes would have been too heavy and bulky and would be very tiring on a long trek. Snow will stick on the outside pair of socks and freeze, which seals them so the others stay dry and warm. We hung up our socks to dry, then we lay down in the bunks and made our plans for the next day. We were very tired, but to some extent excited about the next day as we had only fifteen miles to go. Little did we know how long and terrible those next miles were to be.

In the morning we fixed some breakfast and then cut some wood to replace the wood we had burned so that the next occupants of this cabin would have a welcome sight. It was frigidly cold, about 50 degrees below zero—so cold we chose to wait for daylight to decide whether to start out or not. About 9:30 the first light of dawn shimmered through the frost on the pine trees. Our spirits soared a little with the clear, sharp air, so we packed what food we had left and started down the frozen Peace River. The snow was about a foot-and-a-half deep, and I felt that I was in better condition than Cy so I went ahead and broke trail.

Cy was doing much better than I had hoped for, as his condition was not good even with his weeks of convalescence.

We had eaten all our food by noon so our packs were much lighter, but the steady march was beginning to take its toll on our bodies. The rifles felt like lead weights. Some of the time we would walk on the river and other times along the sides. It was plod along step by step, generally breaking through the upper snow crust and into the deeper powdery crystals below. The river at this point was over a half-mile wide and had a long sweeping curve, so rather than follow it we decided that by crossing and recrossing it, in nearly a straight line, we would be able to save a few miles.

We still had to put up with the vagaries of this huge Arctic stream. When the river first freezes over, the ice is only about two or three inches deep and the water flows fast and full underneath. Then the streams and smaller rivers starting 400 to 500 miles west in British Columbia become smaller when the big freeze slides out of the north. So on the Peace River when the deep cold of forty to fifty below comes, several layers of ice may develop. The top ice on the fast main channel may be only one inch thick, and this gives you quite a shock when you are walking along and you crash down two feet or more, hoping you will hit solid ice. There are other quirks in the swirling water under the ice, which may catch an unwary traveler and plunge him to instant death.

We were beginning to realize that we were in a very precarious situation as fading daylight and distance were "putting on the squeeze." As we crossed the river the first time, we fell through the top shell of ice again and again. Usually, it was me as I was breaking trail. Cy was holding up fairly well so far. We didn't stop to cook some tea since we could see the early afternoon darkness was beginning to set in. We did get across the river the first time before dark, and Cy pointed out a landmark on the other side, which helped us orient ourselves to our position. The darkness was lessened by the reflection off the very white snow. We plodded along and fell through the deep snow and thin top ice on the river hour after hour. The timber wolves started to howl, and we thought they may have smelled us. Perhaps they were assembling a marauding pack for the night. In the back of our minds, we couldn't help but think that they might hunt us down and attack. Sound travels really well in the still cold air. We could hear only the crunch of our steps and then the yips and piercing howls that welled up around us. Those on the side of the river we had left were howling the loudest, but about two miles away we could hear the answering chorus.

We didn't talk much. Surprisingly, the human mind seems to wander under stress. In the dim light we kept glancing at furtive shadows that seemed to skitter amongst the fir trees and poplars. Were they real or only quasi-images of the mind?

I kept the rifle usually in the crook of my left arm so I could be ready to pull off a mitten and fire from the hip. The cold became more penetrating now. We had to make frequent stops so our lungs wouldn't become frost-bitten.

At times I thought of other things. How I owed the hospital ten dollars for the ten-day stay and that I didn't have a cent to pay it. How Orel managed to scrape up the ten bucks was a miracle. But, the Mounties had threatened deportation if I didn't get the money and we knew they meant what they said.

A wolf's howl is very eerie and chilling. We thought things were getting very serious now, so we stopped a few minutes and checked our rifles and shells. We did not say it out loud but we knew in our hearts that this was a time of great danger. We started across the river again, and even though we had the experience of falling through the top shell ice many times before, it was still scary, more so now because it was dark. If we hadn't known how far we were from our destination, we could have become extremely discouraged. We were about a mile away as the crow flies, but we still had a major hazard to overcome. There was open water at several places as it swirled up from below. One miscue and it would be all over. Later, we learned we had walked by the open water without seeing it. Other trappers who had come along later had seen how close we had come. Luck had been on our side. They said we had missed it by about ten feet. It was more like a miracle. It would have been a quick, cold death.

It was at least fifty degrees below zero now. When we finished crossing the river, we came upon another obstacle. We were only about a quarter-mile from the cabin, but there was a hundred-foot bluff in front of us and it was almost straight up.

Since the time Cy had left there to go to the hospital, the other trappers had found a place to scale the bluff. Cy did not know where it was and thus we had to search for a hanging rope he remembered they had left. This proved to be very frustrating. Not wanting to give up when we were so close and wanting so badly to get to the cabin where we would have food and shelter, we kept on searching. Three days of very tough travel and no food since noon had made us desperate. Tired and hungry as we were, with the penetrating cold getting to our bones, it would have been easy to panic, but at this point survival seemed to clarify our thinking. Cy was now in no condition to try, so I started climbing at a place where we both thought it might be possible to make it up the sheer bluff.

I took off my pack, left the rifle with Cy, and told him to wish me luck. I knew, however, it would take more than luck. Grabbing hold of the scrub brush and lower branches of the small trees growing on the cliff face, I climbed about sixty or seventy feet. There was hardly a fingerhold on the rocks above. I stood, gasping for breath, on a narrow ledge feeling my heart pounding with more than exertion. The instinct to live seemed to take over. I paused and thought over the precarious situation. Cy, physically in much worse condition than I was, had to count on me for survival. What if I slip and fall, break a leg, or even get killed as I plunged downward. Cy would certainly freeze to death in the biting cold.

Everything was dark except the nearby snow. I decided I shouldn't go any farther and jeopardize both of our chances. Code of the bush is to stick together and try not to get injured because of foolishness. The cliff had beaten us this time, so I laboriously crept back down, inch by inch, in the darkness.

Chapter 7

Defeat at the Bluff

By Orville

Now we had to decide how to survive the night because even though we were so close, we knew that it was hopeless to try to find the rope or scale that cliff in the dark. We also feared the "sleeping death" that might result if we tried to lay in the snow until morning and unknowingly freeze while we slept.

Cy was a little familiar with the area, for when he and his friends had first come here, they had stayed in an abandoned cabin during the time it took them to build their own. He told me that it was downriver about five or six miles. This would mean shelter, but we would have to walk back another route that he knew. It would add another ten miles to our trip, but we had no other choice. We both envisioned a cabin with a stove in it, a stack of firewood, and maybe someone had left some food there.

So, the decision was made. We would try for it. We would be together, which we now needed very much. Cy was weaker now, but his presence gave me an added strength. The wolves seemed to have stopped howling as they were probably feeding on a fresh kill. Our minds were now concentrated on our objective so strongly that the wolf problem became minor. We kept on walking—trudging would be a more apt way to put it—as we stumbled along in the darkness. We didn't talk unless we stopped to consult each other about whether to go through an island or around it. I think I received additional incentive from Cy as he came plodding along behind me, never complaining. The walk was becoming grueling and unmerciful. My body ached with exhaustion, and the deep cold relentlessly tried to penetrate our bodies. Our lungs seemed to burn from the icy air with every breath. Frost and ice had long before formed on our faces. Potholes and hidden branches caused us to fall time after time in the quasi-darkness. Tree limbs whipped at us, and we had to stop more and more to rest for a few moments. Every bit of our physical reserves were almost at the breaking point. Cy fell more often, but some strong inner force seemed to pick him up and push him on.

Time had been lost to us when we reached the cabin. We could see its blurred, squat shape as we drew near. We stumbled in through the opening where the door had been and were stunned by what we found. In the dim light we could see there were no windows, no stove, nor any food. There was a stack of wood in a corner, so we built a fire on the dirt floor and tried to revive ourselves and absorb some of the radiant heat from the burning sticks. This was at least a shelter. There was no need for us to feel sorry for ourselves. We would make the best of it.

We shed our packs, took off the cloths that we had covered our lower faces with, and scraped together some wild grass we found in a corner, which would keep us off the frozen ground. We had to lay flat in the smoke-filled room so our eyes wouldn't smart so much next to the floor. Our hunger was gnawing at our insides. When we discovered a jar of cracked corn, we tried chewing on some of it, and it helped to have something in our mouths, even though it was pretty much inedible.

We found an empty can and melted some snow, and the hot water tasted good as our tea was gone. We took our rubbers off and our outside pair of socks, which we placed near the fire. In the smoky room, we didn't notice in time to rescue our drying stockings, and they burned up. We finally curled up as close as we dared get to the fire on the dry grass and attempted to sleep.

I woke with a start as the grass we were laying on had caught fire. Cy's cap was on fire, but by slapping my mittens on it, I got the fire out and woke Cy at the same time. We finally got the fire out of the grass and again tried to sleep while still being watchful of the fire, afraid we might burn ourselves severely or fall into such a sleep we would freeze to death. When you are terribly cold, your body responds with great shaking and turning. Your sleep becomes a nightmare of dreams and pain, interspersed with moments of awakening. Your mind cannot rest even though periods of sleep may lull the brain. As I dozed, I thought of how I had started out for this country and the many events since I had left home. At last, we woke to the first light of day and started out for the trappers' cabin.

It was a long, tough climb to move away from the river and up through the hillocks and small valleys in the deep snow to the table land above. It took us about two hours for our tired bodies to reach that area. The sun had just moved above the horizon, even though it must have been around ten o'clock. We were nearing complete exhaustion. Our pauses for rest came more and more often and lasted longer. After about a mile, we came to a path the trappers had been using. It was much easier walking now, and the footprints gave our morale a boost. We would walk ten minutes and then rest about the same length of time. The bright sun seemed to cheer us up a little. We thought of leaving our guns and packs along the trail, but we were still not sure where we were or how far away the cabin was. We ate snow along the way as it quenched our thirst and seemed to help our hunger for a short time. It took a long time to cover a mile. Finally, we could see smoke coming out of the river breaks. Then, after a short distance we looked down over the hill, and there was the cabin. Up until that time, I had not seen anything so beautiful, so welcome. The cabin looked like a fantasy at first, but it was real, for we fired a shot in the air and Cy's friends came running up the hill to greet us. They took our packs and rifles and helped us down the hill. I think we had the Lord watching over us. We began to tell them of our struggles, and by looking at us they would surmise something of what we had been through.

They had a bottle of brandy that they used for emergency purposes, and this they saw was one, so they fixed each of us a hot drink and helped us out of our outside clothing. After we had gotten our clothes off, we sat by the glowing, welcome fire and sipped our brandy. We slowly got up and washed our hands and faces and combed our hair. What a relief. We felt like new men.

We sat down to a table of venison, cold potatoes, and hot coffee. As we ate, we told Cy's friends about our escapades through the fifty miles of wilderness. We hadn't eaten for over twenty-four hours, and we must have looked like gluttons, but they only smiled and pushed more food at us. They treated us like royalty.

The warmth of the cabin, the brandy, and the food relaxed us, and so we proceeded to go to bed. We were sleeping like babies in a minute and didn't wake up until about noon the next day. The trappers had already prepared a big meal for us: venison, potatoes, bread and jam. We ate until we were completely stuffed. After we had finished eating, we sat around and talked while drinking many cups of coffee. We were feeling much better now, so we took a sponge bath and shaved.

After some more languishing by the fire and some welcome relaxation, it was time for supper. We stuffed ourselves again and immediately hit the sack. We slept for twelve hours straight. Now we were really feeling human again. We went outside and walked around to get the stiffness out of our bodies. Later, over a cup of coffee we began to make plans for my return to Peace River.

Dick King, one of the trappers, decided that he had enough trapping for the winter, so he said he would walk back with me. When it came time to go, we made sure we had packed a lot of grub for our journey. Dick also took his share of the furs from this year's season. With our packs, rifles, and furs, we had a heavy load to carry.

Having made three trips before, Dick knew more

about where the cabins along the way were located. We could also save ten miles by lowering ourselves down the bluff with the ropes Cy and I hadn't been able to find before.

The third morning, we started and made it easily to the first cabin. We fixed some supper and then cut up a bunch of firewood. We wanted to get an early start in the morning, so we went to bed early that night. Our plans were to be able to travel about twenty miles a day. It was not as cold now, and we came across some toboggan paths, which made our travels much easier. We got to the Indian cabin shortly after dark. They made room for us and also fixed us supper. Today, we would describe the place as awfully dirty, but if you had walked as far as we had, you too would think it looked as good as a fancy hotel room.

We left in the morning, and as we got nearer to the village of Peace River, we found a good trail to follow. Later, along came a fellow with a team of horses and a sled. What luck! We got a ride the rest of the way into town. It seemed like a godsend. Everything was going our way this time.

When I finally reached home, it seemed unreal to me for some time to come. Here I was, back in our cozy cabin with a happy greeting from Orel. I had covered over one hundred miles of rough wilderness through the use of my feet and willpower. It was good to be young and strong. I thought then that I could overcome any obstacle that came about, but I would never forget the terrible ordeal we had endured as we fought to survive against questionable odds in the rough country of the Peace River.

Orville at the trappers' cabin, recovering from their terrible ordeal on the trek along the Peace River.

Chapter 8

The Last Summer in the North Country
By Orel

During the last summer we spent near Peace River, Orville and I did a variety of work. Bob Claughton, our storekeeper friend, got us a job with the Forest Service fighting fires. We got the first call right away, and six of us left in a power boat for the fire site. We went up the Peace River about twenty miles, set up our camp, and immediately started to fight the fire. We would cut trees down and carry them toward the burning area to start what was called a "fire break" by setting the trees on fire. This would create a burn area back to the main fire and would stop it from moving farther into the forest. We were about to lose control of this big blaze when it started to rain heavily, and our work was completed.

We had plenty of food and had done some fishing, but the river was rising, so somebody got the bright idea to build a raft. Then we were to float on it back to the town of Peace River. We made the raft out of logs, put some pine boughs on it, and began climbing aboard. It could only hold three men, so Reggie Rumlo and I walked along the river bank. We walked to the junction of the Smoky River and the Peace River, where a man by the name of Dutch Neff lived on a farm that was similar to those in Minnesota. He invited us to stay all night, an invitation we were glad to accept, and then he told us he was going to town the next day to pick up his bride-to-be. He had answered a "lonely hearts" ad, and an

English girl and her sister would arrive in Peace River on Thursday. He was going to marry the one, but to get her he had to pay passage for her sister too.

In our conversation that night, he said he would like to get two men to help him build a big raft so he could load pigs on it and ship them to Edmonton, Alberta. Orville and I were both out of work at the time, so we decided to take the job and we were glad to get it.

The next day his wife-to-be and her sister were there on schedule. They were very tall, five feet ten or eleven, about twenty-five and twenty-seven years old, and fair-looking. They talked with a very English brogue. They would walk faster than we could, so I asked them why they walked so fast. One of them said, "You would bloody well get run over in London if you didn't walk fast."

Orville and I rode in the boat with the two girls to Dutch's farm. We milked his cows and came into the house with the milk. Dutch was a little taken back in how to act and what to say, so he brought two small kittens in with him and put them down. Then he took a saucer from the cupboard, poured some milk in it, and put the kittens up to it. One of them walked right into the dish of milk. One of the girls said, "Oh, look. The bloomin' little things are going to take a bloomin' bloody foot bath."

Later, after we had left, Dutch married one of the English gals, but for the present we had to build the big raft for him. We picked up our saws, axes, pry bars, and log chains and went to the river. We took Dutch's boat and went up the river to a big pile of draft logs that had jammed up in a curve of the river. We would crawl onto the pile, cut off the roots, then the top, and keep trimming until we had a log about thirty-five to forty feet long and close to sixteen to twenty inches in diameter. After we had two or three logs ready, we would pull them out into the river, fasten them together with chains, and then pull them back to the farm with the boat. In all, we got about thirty big logs like this and fastened them together into a very stable craft by putting them side by side. We put a big cross log on each end and then we looped wire around each float log and secured them to the cross logs. Our raft turned out to be almost square with a four-foot-high pen on it and a gate on one side.

The third day we started to try to corral the hogs. They were a rangy bunch and could run like heck, but we got most of them, about sixty, into the barn. We would load up about six at a time into a high-wheeled wagon, then back the horses and the wagon into the river so we could unload the hogs onto the raft. We had put spruce boughs and straw down, so the hogs had a nice bed. This operation took us until about four in the afternoon, but in the summer the sun really doesn't set until about ten or eleven o'clock in this country, so the days are really long, and we had plenty of time.

We hooked the raft onto the boat with a big, long, heavy rope and started out with our load of squealing hogs. When Dutch would speed up the boat, the raft would pull down into the water, and then the pigs would squeal more than ever. I wondered how he was going to land this raft in the right place to unload them, but Dutch turned out to be an expert at this.

We fed the hogs some oats that evening and then hauled them to a railroad car the next day. The freight train took them to Edmonton the very next night. At this time the hogs were worth about four cents per pound, and I believe Dutch got about $600 for the lot of them. I never saw Dutch after that, but Orville and Frank Stortz saw him in 1969. He had retired and was living in Peace River.

****

Orville and I got a "hand-out" job from the government in September. We had to cut all the trees on a road grade, which was four rods wide and a mile long, about four acres in the strip. We received $32 for this work, and when this was finished, we helped an older fellow do a similar job. He and his wife boarded us, and we let them keep all of the money because it was a very hard go now for most of the homesteaders during the Depression.

We had previously cut a set of building logs for our barn, forty-four of them forty feet long, and fifty of them were thirty feet long, all peeled and trimmed. We hauled them seven miles to our place but had hardly any money to start the winter, so we decided to sell, which we did. We took off for Peace River, which had been our town for any business or purchases. Niggles had a café in this town, but they had made a fortune in the Klondike Gold Rush by serving meals to the miners. They thought so much of the big stove they had used at that time that they had it hauled back to Peace River. It weighed almost two tons and was about eight feet long with three fire boxes.

One day at the café we thought we would treat ourselves to a good meal, so we ordered pork chops and something else with a long French name. This something turned out to be the last thing we wanted, a cold pancake rolled up with jelly inside. Pancakes were a staple item in the homesteaders' list, and we had had our share.

Peace River had mostly log buildings and all wooden sidewalks. We heard later, after we had left Canada, in a letter from Reggie Rumlo that a fire got started in the winter when it was 54 below, and he said a pail of water would have put the fire out, but everything was frozen up and a lot of the old buildings burned down.

If you liked to skate, Peace River had two ice rinks and a large enclosed curling rink. One of the interesting contests of the town caused lots of interesting predicting. They would hang a light chain from the old ferry cable and let it freeze in the river ice after fastening the other end of the chain to a timer clock. For one dollar, you could wager a guess as to when the ice would break up in the spring. A twelve-year-old boy won $1,600 the first year, but the next spring a lot fewer had bet the dollar as times were never harder than then.

A big occasion for the town was when the first boat came from the north, went to Fort Vermillion with supplies, and brought back about eighty-five trappers with their winter's catch of furs. Some collected as much as $8,000 for their pelts. One trapper would rent every room in the hotel and also the only bar in town, put a fifth of whiskey in every room, and all the beer was free until the saloon closed, which was at ten p.m.

****

A particularly memorable time for Orville was when he worked briefly for Page Rideout, a big rugged man who had the Massey Harris dealership in Peace River. He was from Nova Scotia. The first thing every day, Page would step outside and say, "We are going to have weather."

One morning Page apparently heard the boat whistle, and he excitedly yelled to Orville, "Lord God, crank up that Model T!"

Orville did, and they took off. Page was going pretty fast, and he cut across some lots where he shouldn't have. The crank hooked into a pole anchor that was sticking out of the ground, and Orville and Page sailed right through the windshield and the crank was pulled down under the front axle.

****

Many of the homesteaders could eat well if they kept a garden. With summer sunshine for twenty-one hours a day, stuff grew like it was scared to stay in the ground. Vegetables such as potatoes, onions, cabbage, cucumbers, or any root crop grew twice as fast as they do in southern Minnesota. I helped weigh a head of cabbage that pushed the scales down to forty-four pounds. A hill of potatoes I dug up weighed twenty-three pounds. The common oat yield was one hundred bushels to the acre. Wheat was a touchy crop because it sometimes didn't mature in time with the early frosts in northern Alberta. We had a crop of oats on our farm that yielded 117 bushels to the acre, and the cost of threshing this grain was five cents per bushel. But all we could sell our crop for was seven cents a bushel, and out of that we had to pay for twine and also for having it hauled, so we just gave all of the oats to the thresher to break even. How not to get rich.

The raft that Orel and Orville built to float back to Peace River after fighting the forest fire.

The fire at Peace River. It had been 65 degrees below zero the night before and at noon it was 54 below. Everything was frozen. A pail of water could have put it out, but everything was solid ice.

Chapter 9

Back to the U.S.A.

By Orel

With summer over, we really didn't know what to do as there were no jobs to be had. We heard that another carload of hogs was being loaded to go to Edmonton, so that was possible transportation. We had taken our set of building logs that we had planned to use in building our barn and sold them for $35 so we would have a little money. The buyer said he had only $16, but that he would send us the rest.

We made the big decision. The big freeze was moving down from the Arctic, and it would catch us here if we stayed any longer. We filled our packsacks, oiled our crosscut saws and axes, and left our homey cabin. We had filled the wood box, the water barrel was full, the fire burned cheerily, and the cat was sleeping on the bed when we took a last look and walked out. There was about a foot of snow on the ground, and already it was eighteen degrees below zero. It was the 20th of October.

We said goodbye to our friends and crawled into the railroad car with the hogs. We gathered some straw together and placed it at the end of the car so we would have a place to sleep. During the night a big hog started chasing another, and one of them stepped on Orville's ankle. He was lame for two or three days. By hitching a series of rides on the trains, we got to my Uncle Henry and Uncle John's place at Craik, Saskatchewan, located in the prairie grain belt in the south central area of the province. We had ridden in box cars and on top of the engine water tender, so we were filthy dirty when we arrived.

We ate supper and got into a bed for the first time in three days. My aunt washed our clothes, and we bathed and shaved. We had only eight dollars apiece, even though we had only spent two dollars on the trip, so I asked Uncle Henry for a ten dollar bill because we still had 1,200 miles to go. He said he hadn't had a crop for three years and had only two dollars in his pocket. He had borrowed all he could from the bank and owed $1,300 for taxes due on December 1st.

Uncle Henry had a lot of land, about 5,000 acres with 3,200 of it tillable, but the bad crops had hit him hard. He said, "My credit is still good here, so I will charge some gas and take you to Moose Jaw, where there is a mail train going east at six p.m. and you can try and hop that."

We got on the train but had to ride on top of the water tender. The locomotives at that time were all steam, so we sat on top with the smoke and cinders flying at us so strong that you could hardly see at times. If you've ever had sand thrown in your face, that's the way cinders feel. The train stopped at Estavan for mail delivery and water. We had to be very careful not to be seen, so we sneaked off the tender since the authorities were watching trains and every other vehicle to make sure people didn't cross the border illegally.

We got a room in a Chinese hotel for one dollar, cleaned ourselves up, and went to bed. We got up real early, had some toast and coffee for ten cents, and bought some sardines and crackers for five cents each. We shouldered our packs and started out down the road, but everyone went by us. We walked about four miles until we reached a railroad crossing. While we were sitting there, a section car same along and stopped. The brakeman said, "Get on, and I'll give you a lift for about three miles." He was a talker. He told us that there had been a coal miners' strike and that was probably the reason nobody would give us a ride because we looked like coal miners with our sooty clothes.

After we left the section car, we walked and walked. It grew dark, and we stopped in a schoolhouse and laid down for a rest. We were now getting real hungry, but slept or rested for about two hours and then again started walking in the night toward Portal, where there was a border crossing station into the United States. About midnight we could see the lights of the town. When we finally got there, we were accosted by a huge border guard. We had to answer a lot of questions. Where were we from? Did we have any money? Etc.

We bought a good meal at the railroad station for thirty-five cents. Then the guard escorted us to the hotel and made us register, pay one dollar for the room, and then he told us to report to the immigration office at Portal. When we reported in the next morning, there were many more questions, but they finally let us go.

We started walking. Luck was with us, for we were picked up by a lignite coal hauler with a one-ton 1929 Chevy truck. It was my turn, I guess, for the good spot to ride, so Orville got on top of the load of coal. After we had gone about ten miles, we had to stop as someone had set fire to the slough grass in a big pot hole. The smoke was so bad, an accident had happened. We had no more than stopped when a uniformed officer came up to us and started asking the same questions again. Where did we come from? Where were we going? Etc. After we had talked awhile, we found out that his name was Wackholtz. He said, "Do you know Hoppy Anderson?" I said, "Sure."

He informed us that he was from Winona and that he had played ball against Hoppy at Rushford. As he kept thinking about the Harmony area, he said, "Do you know any Serfliners?"

I replied, "No, but I know some Serflings."

"Name them," he said.

I started with Herman, then Otto and Clarence, and when I came to Harry, he said, "That's the fellow. We were buddies in France."

Wackholtz had a 1929 Model A and said, "Get in. I'm going to Minot to pick up a man."

We were very glad to go with him, and away we went. He took us in for a lunch and offered to lend us some money. We didn't take it as we figured we were almost home.

He said, "There's a good spot outside of Minot to catch a ride. I'll take you there in my car."

At the spot he told us about, we caught a ride in a Model T pickup with no top or windshield. The driver was a Russian fur buyer and sort of a madman also, as he drove his truck wide open against about a forty mile-per-hour wind. When we got to the next town, he said that he knew there was a truck load of calves going to Rugby, North Dakota. When we saw it, the truck had started moving, but we got along side of it and crawled in with the calves.

They were 400-pounders. We sat down on the straw in a corner up front, and as the window in the back of the cab was missing, we could hear the two men in front talking. They were apparently Swedes. They were a rugged, husky-looking pair, but they had no idea they had extra passengers in the back.

Orville couldn't leave well enough alone, as he kept tickling one of the calves. That calf really didn't like someone messing around with him, so he would kick the truck rack behind the cab where there was no glass. We could hear the Swedes say, "Mein Yesus Krist, vat is de matter back der?"

Orville kept doing it again and again. The same story. About the fourth time, the calf was sick of this business and gave a lunge to the back of the truck. The calves were packed in pretty tight, so when the calf lunged, he pooped through the hole where the glass was supposed to be, and it landed on the seat between the two men.

The Swedes broke loudly into their native tongue, stopped the truck, and took the seat out. They got some grass and cleaned off the seat the best they could. They tried to clean their overalls, but it was a stinky mess. Believe me, we laid down close to the straw. There was a wide board along each side, and they didn't see us. We sneaked out of the truck at Rugby before the truck had quite stopped, and the Swedes never knew they had had two tricky Norwegians as unpaid passengers—well, at least one tricky Norske.

When we were walking along the street in Rugby, an unusual thing happened to us. We were going by a filling station, and the owner, an elderly man, stood outside and started to talk to us. He asked us a lot of questions about our destination and where we had come from, and so forth. He said he had lost his wife three weeks before and was very lonesome. He wondered if we would care to come to the house. He said, "I'll lock up and make you some supper, and you might like to clean up."

We welcomed this suggestion after the calf ride and went into the house to wash up the best we could. When we went into his living room and started looking around, I noticed a picture of my Grandpa Felland's house in Harmony, Minnesota, my home town. Grandpa had died in 1918, but my grandmother still lived there. We had a big visit, and he said he had worked once on a farm for Ole Frogner's dad. He fixed us pancakes and sausages for supper, which we really enjoyed. That evening we felt like we had a new lease on life.

Our friend for the evening said there was a big cattle train coming through Rugby at ten p.m. and it would stop for water. He said he knew the conductor and maybe he could get us a ride. When the train arrived, we even got to ride in the caboose provided we would help water the cattle at Breckenridge, which we were very willing to do.

There were five ranchers in the caboose, and among them they owned ninety-six car loads of cattle on the train. They played poker for big stakes, and a tall Scandinavian ended up as the winner. By the time the train reached Wilmar, Minnesota, one of the younger ranchers had lost five car loads of cattle, and he had only one left to pay for his stay in St. Paul and for his ticket home.

We didn't dare ride into St. Paul because the railroad bulls might get us. We had seven dollars left, so we bought bus tickets home to Harmony, leaving us with fifty-five cents between us. The trip took nine hours, and we were really glad to be home. What a welcome sight to see the streets and buildings of Harmony and all of our friends and relatives.

I had lost eight pounds, and Orville didn't fare any better. Our three-year ordeal was over, but we would never forget it. We fully intended to go back to Peace River again, but it was very hard to earn enough to make a return trip. When I could get the work, I would cut wood for one dollar a day. My brother, Eldin, and I cut a two-year supply for our folks. The next spring I hired out to Clarence Haugen for twenty dollars a month with every Sunday night off. This was 1933, and it was very tough for Clarence to pay me. Hogs were two dollars and fifty cents a hundred-weight and cows about the same. Steers brought three or four cents a pound.

We had no regrets about our sojourn in the North Country. We saw the Peace River area as virgin territory before man had encroached upon it a great deal. We took all of the hardships that this wild semi-arctic wilderness could throw at us and survived. With all of its harshness, this was a great place, and our thoughts have returned to this land many times over the years. The great Peace River still flows north, and over time the land has become a beautiful farming development. We think back to our snug little cabin in the woods and wonder if it gave welcome to many strangers. We can see it yet, squat amongst the pines and spruce, while the white smoke from our chimney streams straight up, to finally disappear into the frigid air of northern Alberta.

~ Epilogue ~

The Felland and Severson families grew up hearing the stories of our dads' adventures in the northern Alberta, Canada region. In many ways, the stories seemed like chapters in a fictional tale filled with fun and excitement but also danger, much like the Jack London books that several of us loved to read. And yet the heroes of the Peace River tales were our own fathers! Even though we heard several of the stories numerous times, our dads varied the details enough to keep us interested—or perhaps they, like many of us, remembered events differently over time. Most of the "When we homesteaded in Peace River..." events are told in this book, but there are a few additional stories, along with other versions of the originals, plus updates from succeeding trips to Peace River that family members want to share in this Epilogue. The first three stories are by Jim Felland, followed by Martha Felland's story and remembrances by Rob Severson.

—*Sonja Brown*

One story I remember involved a small job Orel and Orville took on. They had heard about a person who wanted some trees cut, so they headed out from their cabin on foot toward the man's property. On the way, they came upon an Indian camp by the Peace

River. After some visiting back and forth, the Indians invited them to spend the night as it was getting close to dusk. Walking through the camp, Dad saw an Indian boy sitting on a stool with a dead jack rabbit on his lap. The boy was picking the eyes out of it and popping them in his mouth.

Nearby, a woman had a fishing line in the river and was yelling for help. It seems she had a big northern pike on the line and needed help getting it in. None of the men in camp paid any attention to her, so Dad went to give her a hand. Between the two of them, they finally pulled the fish in. Dad said it was huge. The woman took the fish to the chicken yard, chopped the head up, and threw the pieces to the chickens.

Soon, the word got out how big the fish was, and a game warden came to weigh what was left of it. He said that if it had all been there, it probably would have been a world-record catch.

****

Another story was about Dad and Orville trying to find ways to make money. They had talked to a guy in town who owned a restaurant and told them that he had a hard time getting potatoes. So they bought some seed potatoes, planted them, and took care of this garden until the potatoes were ready to harvest. The time came to dig them. Dad and Orville borrowed a team of horses and a wagon, dug the potatoes, and loaded them onto the wagon. By then, it was late in the day, so they decided to wait until morning to take them to their restaurant friend. That night, the temperature dropped to forty degrees below zero, and they lost all of the potatoes.

****

The third story was about their train trip home to Harmony when it seemed no more work was available. A certain passenger Dad and Orville met had filled their ears with a recounting of his success as a homesteader. After a while, this passenger asked the train engineer to stop at a curve near his place, but the engineer said he couldn't do that because the curve was at the start of a long, hard pull. So Dad told the guy to let him know when they were getting close to that location, and he would help him get off. In time, the guy gave the word, so Dad had him stand near the door and gave him a big shove. The last thing Dad and Orville saw was this pair of boots sticking up in the air. They never found out if he was okay.

—*Jim Felland*

****

The Czechoslovakian brothers were neighbors who spoke broken English. They made their living by hunting and trapping beaver and other animals and selling their furs. Often they wore the same set of clothes for weeks at a time. They were single and after a time found themselves lonely for female companionship, so they decided to advertise for wives. Two women from England answered their newspaper ad. After a short correspondence between the two parties, the women agreed to marry the trappers and promptly booked passage to Peace River.

Arriving dressed in long stylish dresses,

the women walked down the gangplank pulling two large trunks. There standing to meet them were the Czechoslovakian brothers in their trappers' skins and fur hats. If you were downwind from them, Dad said, you could smell a foul odor as it had probably been several weeks since they had bathed. The two women stood looking at the men for a few moments, and then the English ladies left with them to become their wives.

—Martha Felland

****

When Tom Severson and I were growing up in Harmony, Minnesota, we frequently heard bedtime stories from our parents. My mother, Evelyn, had spent a summer in Yellowstone National Park in 1929 and often told us about the experience. My dad, Orville, had even more stories about Peace River, which we sometimes found hard to believe, especially the ones involving the seemingly normal winter temperatures of fifty degrees below zero and the wildness of the country. So when Orel and Orville wrote the first edition of this book, we read it with much anticipation. Would we find the tales far-fetched? Our reactions were just the opposite, and we were certain that there was more to the bedtime stories than we had realized. We decided to go to Peace River one day and see the place for ourselves.

In about 1982 Tom and I invited our dad to go with us to Peace River so he could show us around. We flew to Edmonton, Alberta, rented a car, and headed north. It was indeed a long way up to Peace River (about 302 miles), and the country became increasingly rugged over the distance. Dad was able to direct us to the site of the Harmony boys' homestead, although their cabin and other landmarks he remembered were long gone, of course. The town itself had grown over the fifty-plus years from about 1,000 people in the late 1920s to a population of about 6,100 in 1982.

We had fun talking to a number of people Dad had known back then, and their stories about the dances and other events rang true with us. So we walked away convinced that the incredible bedtime stories of our childhood had really happened.

Tom eventually took another trip to Peace

River, this time bringing his family along so they could see the roots of their grandpa's stories. They loved it, especially the chance to meet the couple who remembered the two young homesteaders from southern Minnesota.

A legend of the Beaver Indian tribe, early inhabitants of the area, says, "Drink the water of the Peace River and you will return." Maybe that is true.

—Rob Severson

Whether it's the water or some other element, family members remember the lure of this legendary area for Orel and Orville, who talked often of returning to Peace River. They finally made their dream happen in the late 1970s when they gathered for a reunion of early settlers to reminisce about their homesteading days, which became the inspiration for this book.

Peace
River

About the Authors

Orville Severson (seated) and Orel Felland were lifelong friends who grew up in the southeastern Minnesota town of Harmony in the early decades of the twentieth century just as the Great Depression took hold. Instead of taking the "Go West, Young Man" advice, they headed north to make their fortunes. At least, that was their dream. Reality was a harsh teacher, but they endured and enjoyed the life they found in beautiful Peace River country. Eventually, they returned to the Harmony area where Orville, with his wife, Evelyn, established a fuel oil business and Orel and his wife, Esther, operated a small grocery store in Granger, Minnesota, before purchasing a nearby farm. Both raised families and became involved in many community activities over the years, all the while maintaining their strong friendship and their shared experience of homesteading in Canada. Retiring in the 1970s, Orel began writing a weekly news column for the *Harmony News*. He also wrote a book called *Memoirs and History of Granger*. As for Peace River, he and Orville finally were able to revisit the area, an experience that motivated them to tell their story in this book, first published in 1979 and released by their families in this second edition.

**For more information and for questions
or comments about the book:**

Sonja Brown
P. O. Box 44367
Eden Prairie, MN 55344

SonjaBrown62@gmail.com

www.ingramcontent.com/pod-product-compliance
Lightning Source LLC
Chambersburg PA
CBHW062057280526
45788CB00003B/1268